silly Millies

WORDS

A Computer Lesson

By Jean Haddon
Illustrated by Sharon Vargo

The Millbrook Press
Brookfield, Connecticut

To my computer guys, Brad and Ben,
and to Abby, their savvy sister.
—JRH

To Jean, thanks for the words!
—S.V

Reading Consultant: Lea M. McGee

Silly Millies and the Silly Millies logo are trademarks
of The Millbrook Press, Inc.

Library of Congress Cataloging-in-Publication Data
Haddon, Jean.
Words : a computer lesson / by Jean Haddon;
illustrated by Sharon Vargo.
p. cm.
Summary: While their parents are out, a big brother is supposed to
be teaching his baby sister computer terms but he is involved in video
games and doesn't notice her following his directions to the letter.
ISBN 0-7613-2870-X (lib. bdg.) ISBN 0-7613-1797-X (pbk.)
1. Reading (Early childhood)—Juvenile literature.
2. Computers—Juvenile literature. [1. Reading (Primary)
2. Computers. 3. Vocabulary.] I. Vargo, Sharon Hawkins, ill. II. Title.
LB1139.5.R43 H33 2003
372.4—dc21 2002009156
Published by The Millbrook Press
2 Old New Milford Road
Brookfield, Connecticut 06804
www.millbrookpress.com

Printed in the United States of America
5 4 3 2 1 (lib.)
5 4 3 2 1 (pbk.)

11

17

Program

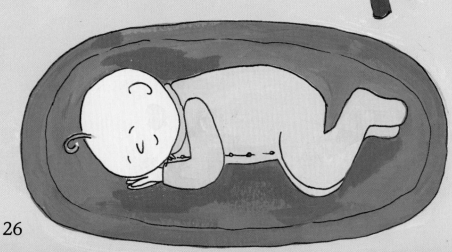

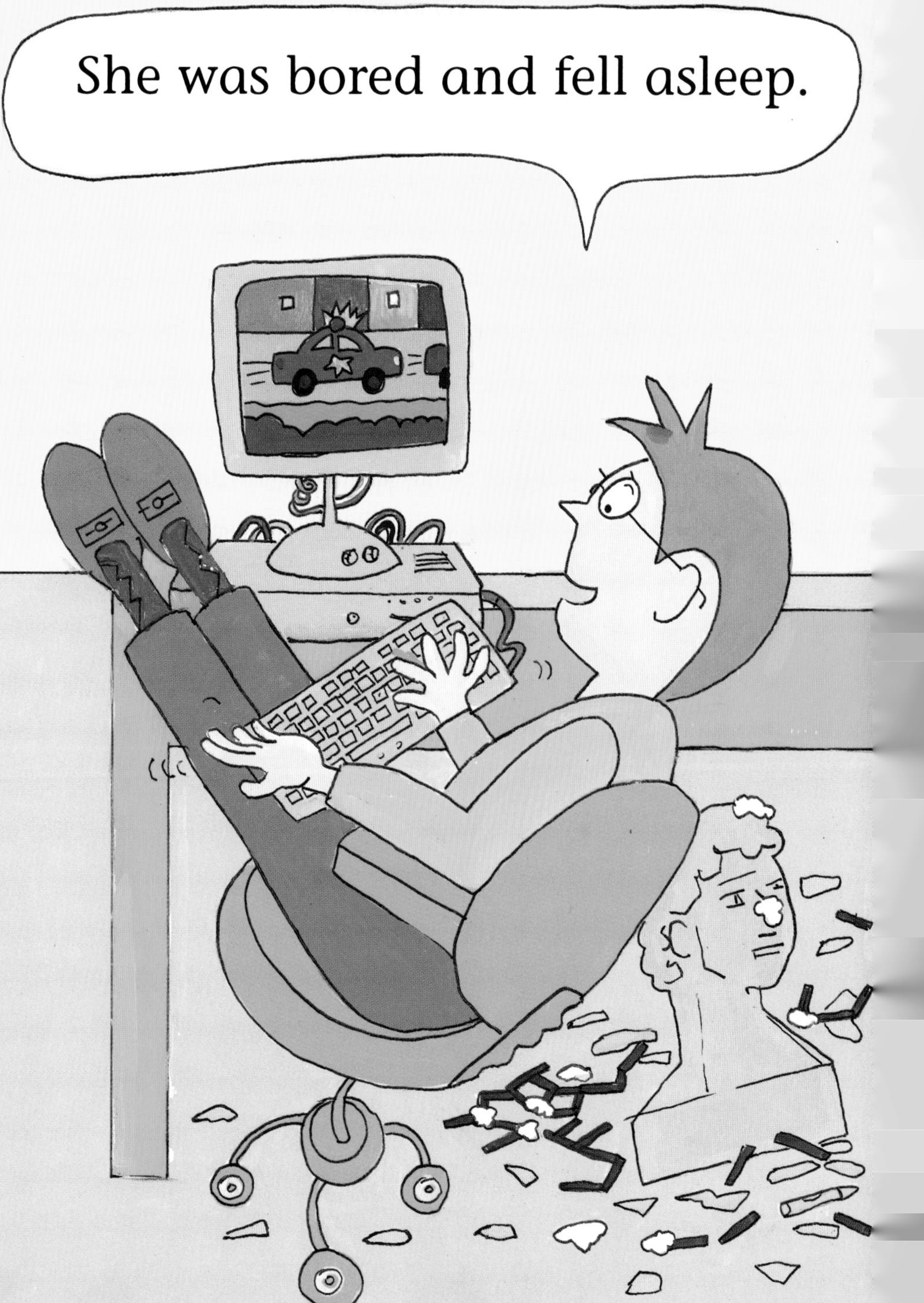
She was bored and fell asleep.

30

Dear Parents:

Congratulations! By sharing this book with your child, you are taking an important step in helping him or her become a good reader. The simple text of *Words: A Computer Lesson* is perfect for the child who is learning the alphabet and is interested in books but can not yet read alone.

Tips for Reading

- First, before reading the book invite your child to look through the book and talk about the pictures. Then read the book aloud to your child. Point to each word as you read it. Stop and talk about the pictures on each page. Talking about what the story is about is one of the MOST important parts of reading. If your child is at all familiar with computer terms, he or she will understand the jokes.
- Reread the book again, pausing to let your child join you in saying the word that goes with the picture.
- Reread the book often, letting your child say as many of the words as possible. Soon your child will know the book so well, he or she will be able to say the words from memory. Keep pointing to the words as you read together. Invite your child to point to the words, too! This is the second MOST important part of reading. Children need to match the printed words with the words they remember about the story.
- Most of all, enjoy the funny story together!

Tips for Discussion

- See if your child recognizes any of the computer toolbar words. If not, can he or she guess what the commands might do?
- Some of the words (*run, table, save,* for example) provide a springboard for a discussion of common words that have more than one meaning.
- Using the fact that there is a story you read and another story you see, discuss the role of pictures in a book. How do you find reading clues in the pictures?

Lea M. McGee, Ed.D.
Professor, Literacy Education
University of Alabama